100+ Instant Writing Tips …

100+
Instant Writing Tips ...
to help you steer clear of wrong turns and give your readers a smooth ride

Norm Friedman

Dash Press
Cleveland, Ohio

Printed in the United States of America

Dash Press
23702 Duffield Road
Cleveland, Ohio 44122

ISBN: 978-0-578-10337-2

First Edition: April 2012

10 9 8 7 6 5 4 3 2 1

Book design by Jason Plapp

www.normfriedman.com

Contents

ACKNOWLEDGMENTS

I must begin with heartfelt thanks to my wife Lynne for all her love and encouragement … and trust that I could finish a project containing no deadline. I am glad one of us had that faith.

Thank you to my son-in-law Jason, who lent so much expertise and care to the book's design.

And I salute my editorial board of children, siblings, cousins, friends, and colleagues—able writers and fabulous people every one—who reacted to my first draft with outstanding suggestions.

WHAT THIS BOOK IS

Today, most of our written communication is immediate. Whether we're emailing a response to a customer's question three minutes after receiving it or texting a friend we just saw at lunch, the emphasis is on speed. But as we make immediacy our priority, writing standards can suffer.

So has polishing our writing become less important? I say, "No." Taking a few precautions to help ensure correctness enhances our credibility and keeps readers focused on what we're saying—not the errors in the way we said it. Clarity and brevity give readers appreciation of a writer who invests some thought and discipline before pressing *Send.* Vivid language and a pleasing tone increase the chances that our message will make an impact.

Recognizing that we need to do more than just *hope* the pendulum will swing back toward more conscientious writing—and believing that most of us care about the impression we make when we write—I decided to do my part in nudging the pendulum by creating a handbook of quick, practical tips for today's writer. I hope you find it useful.

WHAT THIS BOOK ISN'T

This book is not scientific. I didn't analyze any data or canvass scholars to come up with my top 100 tips. Instead, the pointers are based on years of observing workplace writing, years of writing and editing, and years of conducting writing workshops for various employee groups.

You won't see much about *prepositions* or *participles* in this book, and you won't find *gerund* at all. I did not want this guide to resemble a schoolbook, but once in a while I needed a term like *idiom* to make a point. I apologize.

BON VOYAGE

Before you enter your on-ramp to more error-free and confident writing, I offer four recommendations about your overall approach:

- Be the reader. The more you identify with the reader in deciding what to include and how to express yourself, the better your writing.
- Build an ever-expanding repertoire of favorite words and phrases that enable you to write with precision and polish.
- Build an ever-expanding alarm system to warn you of tricky situations. The following pages should help you set a number of new alarms.
- Know that rewording to avoid a thorny grammar or punctuation issue is not wimpy. It's smart.

Have fun and drive safely.

NAVIGATING TRICKY INTERSECTIONS

Uh-oh. Two similar words or phrases are on a collision course in your brain. Which one has the right-of-way?

Tip #1

Do you *hone in* or *home in*? Don't confuse *hone* (meaning *sharpen*) with *home in* (meaning *zero in*—like a homing pigeon).

> **This book is aimed at honing writing skills.**
> **This book homes in on dozens of common writing errors.**

Tip #2

If you hint at something, you aren't *inferring*; you're *implying*. When the sender of a message *implies*, the receiver needs to *infer* the meaning.

> **When our CEO implied that a major change was afoot, I inferred that the rumors of a merger were true.**

+ So when you *make an inference*, you're on the receiving end of a communication.

Tip #3

Use *number* when referring to individual items that can be counted and *amount* when referring to a quantity that is expressed as a whole.

> **What amount of money did you have in mind?**
> **I was surprised at the number of dollar bills in the tip jar.**

+ Note that *money* is singular and *bills* is plural. The common error is using *amount* with a plural word. So it's *number* of light bulbs or *number* of responses, not *amount.*

Tip #4

Use *fewer* when referring to individual items that can be counted and *less* when referring to a quantity that is expressed as a whole.

> **We wound up at a restaurant with fewer windows and less ambience.**

+ You shouldn't write or say *less* windows, but common phrases like *25 words or less* are acceptable as idioms. That means you don't have to scoot up a ladder and yank down those grocery check-out signs that say *12 items or less.*

Tip #5

Don't write *principle* when you mean *principal.* We know that a *principle* is a belief, idea, rule, ethic, etc., but we sometimes forget that *principal* has many meanings.

> **You'll never see Lynne compromise her principles.** (Her values or moral code.)
> **Increased competition looms as our principal challenge.** (Adjective meaning *primary, main,* or *chief.*)
> **Dan has been a principal of our firm since 2001.** (One of the heads of the company.)

Our children's principal always takes a cameo role in the school production. (Head of the school.)
We succeeded in cutting our loan's principal by 20 percent this year. (The amount borrowed.)
Shelley lives off the interest from her inheritance, never invading the principal. (The amount invested.)

Tip #6
Distinguish between *everyday* and *every day*. It helps if you recognize that *everyday* is an adjective while *every day* functions as an adverb.

For Robert, saying something politically incorrect is an everyday event.
My boss seems to start a new diet every day.

+ If knowing an adjective from an adverb isn't second nature, note that *everyday* will commonly precede the word it's describing (an *everyday* problem; your *everyday* jacket).

Tip #7
Affect is usually a verb meaning to influence; *effect* is usually a noun meaning the result of that process.

We hoped the new office policy would affect morale.
We never dreamed the new office policy would have such an immediate effect.

+ Are you wondering why I said *usually* a verb and *usually* a noun? At the end of this book, you'll find *GPS Guidance* on a few particularly challenging issues, and the *affect-effect* dilemma is #1. Check it out if you want to know more.

Tip #8

Historical and *historic* are different. *Historical* signifies merely that something happened in the past or relates to history. *Historic* means momentous—deserving of a place in history.

> **Jean's report was mainly historical.**
> **This is a historic day for our school.**

+ Maybe you expected me to write *an historic day*, so let's clear this up. Yes, when the *h* is silent we do say or write *an herb garden* or *an heir to the throne*. But although we'd never say or write *an hearing aid* or *an hillside*—because the *h* is heard—some of us use *an historic* instead of *a historic*. Is *an* wrong? No. Is it necessary? No. When the *h* is heard, but the accent is on the second syllable (as in *historic* or *habitual*), *a* and *an* are both correct. But I recommend sticking with *a* whenever you hear the *h* sound to make life simpler.

Tip #9

Criteria isn't both singular and plural. It's plural. Remember to use *criterion* when you are referring to only one standard or measure.

> **Except for the criterion of getting off to a prompt start, the meeting was outstanding.**
> **Let's rank the candidates on six criteria.**

+ Handle *phenomenon* (singular) and *phenomena* (plural) the same way.

Tip #10

Drastic has extreme and negative connotations, so it sounds odd when emphasizing something positive (a *drastic improvement*). *Dramatic* usually substitutes well (along with *marked* or *significant*).

> **Ruth spearheaded dramatic strides in efficiency.**
> **Our budget requires that we make drastic cuts in programming.**

Tip #11

Do you *lie* on the couch to watch TV, or *lay* there? Your ear won't help you much because so many of us get this wrong in speech and in writing. You *lie* on the couch, but you *lay* a pillow on it. The difference is that *lie* is the verb for resting in a prone position while *lay* is the verb for setting something down.

> **I just want to lie here and read.**
> **The village lies serenely at the foot of rugged mountains.**
> **Just lay your keys on the counter.**

+ Grammar alert: Sorry to get sticky, but if you happen to be among the few who recognize the difference between a *transitive* verb and an *intransitive* one, your knowledge will help greatly here. Because *lay* takes an object, like *pillow* or *keys*, it is a *transitive* verb, meaning there is a recipient of the action. *Lie* is *intransitive* because you can't *lie* something.

++ For more on this troublesome verb pair, go to GPS #2.

Tip #12

The primary meaning of *disinterested* refers to impartiality (no vested interest in the outcome); use *uninterested* when describing someone who just isn't interested.

> **As a disinterested party, Fran facilitated the discussion.**
> **Les was uninterested in the findings.**

Tip #13

Do you *peak* interest or *pique* it? You want *pique*—meaning *arouse* or *awaken*.

> **Our new neighbor's unusual hours have piqued my curiosity.**
> **My curiosity reached its peak when our new neighbor washed his car at midnight.**

Tip #14

Distinguish between *compliment* (or *complimentary*)—related to a favorable comment—and *complement* (or *complementary*)—related to enhancement or fitting together.

> **I am eager to see Joe and compliment him on his speech.**
>
> **Katie often overhears complimentary remarks about her white hair.**
>
> **I bought special stamps to complement the elegance of the envelope.**
>
> **The family room colors are striking individually, but they're not complementary.**

+ Keeping *compliment* and *complement* straight is easier if you note the tie between *complement* (or *complementary*) and the idea of completeness.

++ Another meaning for *complement*, pertaining to a total or allowance, is often preceded by *full.*

> **Our department is back at its full complement.**

+++ *Complimentary* also means free (*complimentary* tickets).

++++ To *compliment* someone is considered more sincere than to flatter.

Tip #15

Is it *I finally decided who to send to the conference* or *I finally decided whom to send to the conference*? It's *whom*, and here's a slick trick to help get it right.

First rearrange the key words: *I finally decided to send ____ to the conference*. Now choose *he* or *him* to fill the blank, knowing that *he* aligns with *who* (no *m* in either word), and *him* aligns with *whom* (*m* in both words). Your ear will yield the answer. You'd never say or write *send he to the conference*, but *send him* sounds natural and correct. Voila! Because the answer is clearly *him*, the word you want is *whom*.

I finally decided whom to send to the conference.

+ In informal writing you might not need to go through all this problem-solving because many readers don't notice when *who* is wrong, or don't care. But if you care, go to GPS #3.

Tip #16

In lieu of means *in place of*. Don't confuse it with *in light of* or *in view of*.

Corie was quite pleased with our contribution in lieu of a gift.

We postponed the canoe trip in light of the iffy forecast.

In view of our new intern's shyness, I introduced him to one person at a time.

Tip #17

Irregardless is not an acceptable word; use *regardless*—or, in many cases, *irrespective*.

I say that regardless (or *irrespective*) **of the unfortunate rumors, Flanagan will win the election.**

Tip #18

Averse means opposed (to) and applies to people's attitudes. *Adverse* means unfavorable or difficult and applies to situations or conditions.

If no one is averse to the idea, let's ask Shayna to chair the project.

Despite adverse weather, the plane arrived on time.

Tip #19

Keeping *e.g.* and *i.e.* straight is a lot easier once you know a trick for each.

Think of *e.g.* as having the same sound as *egg*, the initial sound in *example*, because another way of saying *for example* is *e.g.*

> **They have traveled to a number of exotic places (e.g., Iceland, Argentina, and New Zealand).**

Think of *i.e.* as being an abbreviation for *in essence*.

> **HR is studying our firm's compensation disparities (i.e., male vs. female salaries).**

In the first instance, *e.g.* (from the Latin *exempli gratia*, meaning *for the sake of example*) leads into examples of the exotic places. In the second, *i.e.* (from the Latin *id est*, meaning *that is*) leads into what is really meant by the compensation disparities.

Tip #20

Comprised of is gaining acceptance because of frequent usage, but the phrase rankles readers who know that *of* doesn't really belong with *comprise*. Go with *composed of* or *consists of* (or just *comprises* for readers who will know you didn't make a mistake).

> Not recommended: **Our department is comprised of seven full-time employees and two part-time interns.**
>
> Recommended: **Our department is composed of** (or *consists of*) **seven full-time employees and two part-time interns.**
>
> Recommended: **Our department comprises seven full-time employees and two part-time interns.** (You can think of *comprises* as meaning *is made up of*.)

Tip #21

Don't call a group or delegation a *contingency*; it's a *contingent*. Use *contingency* when something is uncertain or unpredictable.

> **Although our contingent was small, it was one of the most influential at the convention.**
>
> **We thought we had planned for every contingency, but we still had some hectic moments.**

+ You can also express uncertainty with the phrase *contingent on*.

> **Going ahead with the meeting is contingent on our consultant's schedule.**

Tip #22

Orientate, administrate, and *preventative* are all in the dictionary, but *orient*, *administer*, and *preventive* are less clunky and preferred.

> **Can we orient the volunteers in two hours?**
>
> **Assuming we get funding for the project, who will administer it until we hire a director?**
>
> **If we had taken just a few preventive measures, we'd have turned a profit.**

+ *Towards* is another acceptable word that is not preferred. Use *toward*.

Tip #23

Use *all right* instead of *alright*, which is marginally acceptable at best. Don't even think about using *alot* instead of *a lot*.

> **The collision at home plate was scary, but our catcher is all right.**
>
> **We found a lot of fossils on our hike.**

Tip #24

Do you take a different *tack* or *tact*? It's *tack*, as in the sailing term referring to direction. And we know *tact* is diplomacy.

> **Trying the new <u>tack</u> of emphasizing our customer service has boosted sales.**
>
> **I was impressed with your masterful <u>tact</u> at the board meeting.**

+ Make sure to spell *intact* (complete or not damaged) as one word.

> **The IT wizards fixed my computer, and all my files are <u>intact</u>.**

Tip #25

Farther and *further* can be hard to separate, but if you reserve *farther* for references to physical distance and otherwise use *further*, you should be fine.

> **The drive to the inn was <u>farther</u> than we had anticipated.**
>
> **I understood the poem up to a point and then couldn't get any <u>further</u>.**

Tip #26

Knowing when to use *that* and when to use *which* is not as difficult as you might think—despite the length of this tip. Use *that* to introduce a section of the sentence that is essential for clarity. Use *which* to introduce something non-essential. (Because the section is non-essential, it needs to be set off by punctuation.)

> **The tree <u>that</u> toppled during the ice storm was more than 60 years old.**
>
> **My parents' cherry tree, <u>which</u> they planted when they bought their house, barely survived the ice storm.**

In the first sentence *that toppled during the ice storm* is essential. It identifies the tree. In the second sentence *which they planted when they bought their house* adds interesting detail, but it is not essential. The tree has been identified as the cherry tree.

+ Because *that* can be deleted whenever a sentence is just as clear without it, pay particular attention to each *that* when proofing.

  The film that we saw at the festival was spellbinding. (No need for *that*.)

++ Prefer *who* over *that* when referring to a person.

  Acceptable but impersonal: **Morry is the one that caught the error.**

  Better: **Morry is the one who caught the error.**

+++ *Which* can sound more formal or elegant than *that* and is often found in legal writing, citations, etc.—probably for that reason—when *that* would be correct.

++++ Obviously, *that* and *which* are used in other ways that cause no confusion.

  I want that shirt.

  Which car is yours?

Tip #27

Resist the temptation to put an apostrophe in *its* when you want the possessive form. *It's*, of course, is a contraction for *it is* or *it has*.

  I remember the hotel well, but not its name. (Possessive.)

  It's a shame we had a low turnout. (Contraction for *It is*.)

  It's been two years since I saw Lenore. (Contraction for *It has*.)

+ To resist the impulse to put an apostrophe in the possessive pronoun *its*, remember that no possessive pronouns contain apostrophes—and many have an *s*. Think *ours, his, hers, theirs, yours*.

Tip #28

Don't write *your* as the contraction for *you are*.

Ouch: **You haven't let me know if <u>your</u> coming to the party.**

Right: **You haven't let me know if <u>you're</u> coming to the party.**

+ Take the same care with *whose* and *who's*.

<u>Whose</u> car are we taking? (Possessive.)

<u>Who's</u> meeting me at the station? (Contraction for *Who is*.)

Two keys to brevity are investing more time in organizing your message and resisting the urge to include marginal information. A third key is expanding your mental catalog of unnecessary words and phrases that lengthen the reader's journey. Here is a starter kit.

Tip #29

Cut the fat by using *because* instead of *due to the fact that*, *to* instead of *for the purpose of*, *about* (or *regarding*) instead of *in regard to*, and *to* instead of *in an effort to* and *in order to*.

> **Because** (not *Due to the fact that*) **three team members were out Friday, the meeting has been reset for Tuesday at 10.**
>
> **We are forming a task force to study** (not *for the purpose of studying*) **our minority outreach.**
>
> **I'd like to see you about** (not *in regard to*) **your recycling suggestion.**
>
> **We initiated Friday breakfasts to** (not *in an effort to*) **build camaraderie.**
>
> **You can delete the chart to** (not *in order to*) **fit everything on one page.**

Tip #30

Prune redundant pairs like *goals and objectives*, *pleased and delighted*, and *devoted and dedicated*. They may sound grand, but the discriminating reader will see the fat.

> **Our grant application needs more clearly stated <u>objectives</u>** (or *goals*).
>
> **We are <u>pleased</u>** (or *delighted*) **to invite you to serve on this year's Nominating Committee.**
>
> **Max is an exceptionally <u>devoted</u>** (or *dedicated*) **volunteer in our after-school program.**

Tip #31

Avoid common redundancies like *consensus of opinion*, *past experience*, and *safe haven*.

> **The <u>consensus</u> is that we should change the date of the seminar.**
>
> **Do you have <u>experience</u> working with seniors?**
>
> **Hundreds of flood victims have gratefully found a <u>haven</u> at the community center.**

+ Note that phrases like *consensus of opinion* and *safe haven*, in addition to being redundant, dilute the expressive power of great words. *Consensus* and *haven* deserve to stand on their own.

Tip #32

One of the most common redundancies is *period of time*. It's as if the phrase has become a word, but all we need is *period* or *time*, not both.

> **Nolan served as marketing director for a <u>period</u>** (or a *time*) **and then became a VP.**

+ *Point in time* is similar; use *point* or *time*.

> **At this <u>point</u>** (or *time*) **I really can't speculate.**

Tip #33

Watch out for redundancies when you use verbs beginning with *re-*.

No: **My grandchildren like to hear me reflect back on my childhood.**

Yes: **My grandchildren like to hear me reflect on my childhood.**

No: **Let's not revert back to last month's production problems.**

Yes: **Let's not revert to last month's production problems.**

No (unless this will be the third explanation): **Please repeat your explanation again.**

Yes: **Please repeat your explanation.**

Tip #34

Sentences that begin with *The reason* do not then need *because* or *why*.

No: **The reason I didn't stay for his speech was because I had already heard him on the radio.**

Worse: **The reason why I didn't stay for his speech was because I had already heard him on the radio.**

Fine: **The reason I didn't stay for his speech was that I had already heard him on the radio.**

+ Note that we are most concise when we just eliminate *The reason* and use *because*.

I didn't stay for his speech because I had already heard him on the radio.

++ In the middle of a sentence, use either *reason* or *why*, not both.

No: **I don't understand the reason why my cousin won't lend me money.**

Yes: **I don't understand the reason my cousin won't lend me money.**

Yes: **I don't understand why my cousin won't lend me money.**

Tip #35

Positive and *negative*—often used redundantly—belong on your radar. You don't need them in phrases like *positive strides* or *negative losses.*

> **I'm proud to announce a positive breakthrough.** (Strike *positive.*)
> **The neighborhood has experienced a negative decline.** (Strike *negative.*)

+ *Positive* and *negative* often appear in phrases that could be stated in one word. Instead of *positive outcomes*, you might use *advances* or *achievements*; *negative effects* might be *setbacks* or *damage.*

Tip #36

Save words by using *meet* instead of *hold a meeting*, *decide* instead of *make a decision on*, and *consider* instead of *give consideration to.*

> **Let's meet** (not *hold a meeting*) **to fine-tune the proposal.**
> **We need to decide** (not *make a decision on*) **who's representing us at the conference.**
> **Anna suggested we consider** (not *give consideration to*) **Jeff as our liaison.**

Tip #37

Beware of fat phrases like *the state of Maryland*, *large in size*, *red in color*, and *the month of August.* Just go with *Maryland*, *large*, *red*, and *August.*

> **Emma covers Maryland** (not *the state of Maryland*) **and D.C.**
> **Their patio is quite large** (not *large in size*).
> **The quilt is mainly red** (not *red in color*).
> **We usually go on vacation in August** (not *the month of August*).

+ Four words that commonly lead us astray are *existence*, *occurrence*, *nature*, and *basis.*

Chubby: **You couldn't help noticing the existence of tension.**
Slimmed down: **You couldn't help noticing the tension.**
Chubby: **A traffic jam in our sleepy town is a rare occurrence.**
Slimmed down: **A traffic jam in our sleepy town is rare.**
Chubby: **If your call is of an urgent nature, please contact Kirk at extension 116.**
Slimmed down: **If your call is urgent, please contact Kirk at extension 116.**
Chubby: **I monitor my aunt's bank accounts on a regular basis.**
Slimmed down: **I regularly monitor my aunt's bank accounts.**

Tip #38

Watch out for *both* followed by *same* or *different*.

Redundant: **We both went to the same high school.**
Concise: **We went to the same high school.**
More informative: **We both went to Wilson High.**
Redundant: **Although they are identical twins, Deborah and Bonnie are both into different sports.**
Concise: **Although they are identical twins, Deborah and Bonnie are into different sports.**

+ Watch out for needlessly using the word *both* when it erroneously implies *two*.

Misleading: **We invited both physicians and dentists to the seminar.** (Mid-sentence, the reader thinks two physicians were invited.)
Clear: **We invited physicians and dentists to the seminar.**

++ Using *both* is especially effective in expressing contrast.

The speaker was both analytical and humorous.

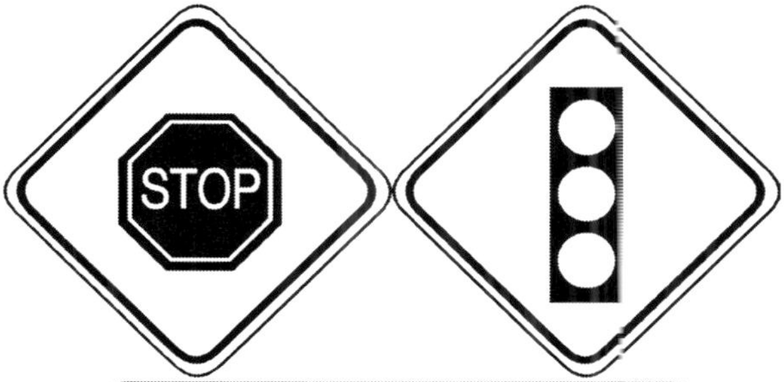

HEEDING SIGNS AND TRAFFIC LIGHTS

Proper use of punctuation prevents your reader from skidding off the road. Periods tell the reader to come to a complete stop. Colons act like bridges. Dashes can alert the reader to a minor detour. Here are a few tips on helping your reader travel effortlessly through your message.

Tip #39

Don't use a comma to separate what qualifies as two complete sentences. This fundamental error is called a *comma splice* or *comma fault*. You can correct the mistake several ways.

> No: **Dennis ran the morning session, his associate took over in the afternoon.**
>
> Yes: **Dennis ran the morning session; his associate took over in the afternoon.**
>
> Yes: **Dennis ran the morning session. His associate took over in the afternoon.**
>
> Yes: **Dennis ran the morning session, and his associate took over in the afternoon.**
>
> Yes: **After Dennis ran the morning session, his associate took over in the afternoon.**

+ If using a semicolon as above is not in your repertoire, you might be concerned that this lack of artistry will impede your path to the Pulitzer Prize. No need to worry. As you see, you have several ways to avoid a comma splice. But if you would like to add this bit of flair, here are the rules:

- The two sections you want to separate with a semicolon need to be *independent clauses* (complete thoughts).
- The sections should be highly related—so much so that they seem to belong in the same sentence.
- The sections should not be joined with *and* or *but*; you don't need a conjunction because the semicolon simultaneously shows a grammatical separation and a contextual connection.

Tip #40

How many commas do you need in this sentence?

> **The panel examined all the responses from community members living in the suburbs and concluded that their comments were strikingly similar to those of city residents.**

You don't need any. Yes, the sentence is somewhat lengthy, but let's break it down. The *subject* is *panel.* Everything after that is the *predicate*, explaining what the panel did, and in this instance no part of the predicate needs punctuation. A comma after *suburbs* would interrupt the flow and be incorrect.

+ Although the sentence above is correct, you might want to reword it to give the reader a break midway.

> **After examining all the responses from community members living in the suburbs, the panel concluded that their comments were strikingly similar to those of city residents.**

Tip #41

When you use a comma to set off a part of the sentence that is not essential, don't forget the second comma.

Oops: **Zack, our former bookkeeper is studying architecture.**

Got it: **Zack, our former bookkeeper, is studying architecture.**

Tip #42

When addressing the person you are writing, put punctuation around the name.

Thank you, Gretchen, for bailing me out yesterday.

+ For the above reason many emails start in error—although the crime is hardly serious.

Not quite right: **Hi Gretchen,**

I finally have your answer.

Right: **Hi, Gretchen.**

I finally have your answer. (Because Gretchen is being addressed directly, her name should have punctuation on both sides.)

Tip #43

Some rules on using commas require discretion. It would be clumsy, for example, to use a comma in an extremely short *compound sentence* (a sentence with a subject and verb and another subject and verb).

Ray drove and Leslie flew. (A comma after *drove* would be correct because this is a compound sentence, but the comma is not necessary.)

Jessup tapped Elizabeth, and Janie offered to help her. (This compound sentence isn't long either, but without the comma the reader will momentarily think Jessup tapped two people.)

Tip #44

When specifying a date that includes the year, remember that you need punctuation before and after the year.

> **The first conference was held on June 11, 1998, in Atlanta.**

+ If you are stating just the month and year, use no comma.

> **The first conference was held in June 1998 in Atlanta.**

Tip #45

When naming a city and state, don't forget that you need punctuation after the state.

> **We chose Akron, Ohio, as the site of our next family reunion.**

Tip #46

Commas and periods always go inside quotation marks—even when logic would dictate otherwise.

> **I don't think there is a word "flustrated," but maybe there should be.**
>
> **I remember that Greg said he felt "woozy."**

+ An absolute rule that doesn't seem to make sense can come across as bad news, but maybe it's good news. Now you never have to take the time to apply reason to these two situations. Whenever a period or comma strays outside the quotation marks, make like a sheepdog and herd the period or comma inside.

++ If you are skeptical about commas and periods always going inside quotation marks and want to look for proof, check any newspaper, magazine, or book—as long as it was published in the U.S. The British style is different, which demonstrates the arbitrariness of this punctuation rule.

+++ Up to now, to give the book a cleaner look, I have been using italics for many words I would normally surround with quotation marks. In this section, however, I am deviating from the established style of the book because quotation marks are the focus of tips 46–48. We will return to your regular programming in tip #49.

Tip #47

Question marks and exclamation points can go inside or outside quotation marks, depending on the relationship of the punctuation mark to the section in quotes. Trust your logic.

> **Did you say our photocopier is "over the hill"?**
> **Mike asked, "How long should a photocopier last?"**
> **Stop calling me a "doofus"!**
> **Sue yelled, "Help me!"**

Tip #48

Semicolons and colons always go outside quotation marks (which is logical).

> **She called her absence a "personal day"; I guess to her the World Series is personal.**
> **Four of our culinary students are competing in the "Souper Bowl": Kelly, Hannah, Mo, and John.**

Tip #49

If an entire sentence is in parentheses, the final punctuation goes inside them. If just a section is parenthetical, the final punctuation goes outside. Trust your logic.

> **Karen was elected president of the school board. (Her mom served in the same capacity 32 years ago.)**
> **Karen's mother also headed the school board (32 years ago).**

Tip #50

Don't insert an apostrophe when pluralizing a name; names are pluralized in the same way as other words.

Wrong: **We invited the Brown's to our open house.**
Right: **We invited the Browns to our open house.**
Wrong: **We invited the Ross's to our open house.**
Right: **We invited the Rosses to our open house.**

+ When a first or last name ending in *s* is singular and possessive, the *s* that normally follows the apostrophe is optional. Determine your style and stick with it.

Correct: **I found Phyllis's report.**
Also correct: **I found Phyllis' report.**
Correct: **I found Cathy Jones's report.**
Also correct: **I found Cathy Jones' report.**

++ When a last name is plural and possessive, make the name plural and then add the apostrophe.

Did you see the Smiths' new car?
Did you see the Walshes' new car?
Did you see the Joneses' new car?

Tip #51

Is it *Al and Susan's* or *Al's and Susan's*? The answer is logical.

We went to Al and Susan's home. (One home, jointly owned.)
We borrowed Al's and Susan's bicycles. (Two bikes, his and hers.)

Tip #52

Exclamation points should be used with discretion so they retain impact. And multiple exclamation points should be used rarely—in extremely informal writing—or never.

Over-the-top: **I can't believe what Mickey proposed at the meeting!!!**
Acceptable: **I can't believe what Mickey proposed at the meeting!**
Professional: **I can't believe what Mickey proposed at the meeting.**

+ An exclamation point can reflect that we are struggling to give a statement added impact. Instead of slapping down an exclamation point to compensate for minimal effort, add detail or beef up the language.

Commonplace: **We had great weather!**
Compelling: **We enjoyed seven radiant days and never put on a jacket.**

Tip #53

An ellipsis (three dots) signifies a pause, omission, or lack of completeness. Sometimes an ellipsis will look as if it has four dots because the extra dot is the period at the end of a sentence, but a true ellipsis never has five dots or eight—just as an exclamation point should always be limited to one. We need to contain our exuberance.

David said, "I do remember you. You're … Sherry." (The ellipsis signifies a pause while David racks his brain.)

The senator said, "Our citizens committee … has made three outstanding recommendations." (The ellipsis signifies an omission in the quote.)

To be continued … (The ellipsis signifies incompleteness.)

I guess this will have to be continued.… (The ellipsis signifies incompleteness, but here the statement meets the requirements of a full sentence, so we have a period and an ellipsis.)

+ The spacing before, inside, and after an ellipsis varies from publication to publication. You're safe going with the look you like.

Everyone in the program spoke eloquently…except the guest speaker.
Everyone in the program spoke eloquently … except the guest speaker.
Everyone in the program spoke eloquently . . . except the guest speaker.

Tip #54

Just because you sometimes see a hyphen between two words, such as *follow-up*, don't stick a hyphen there automatically. Think about the usage.

Functioning as an adjective: **I made 14 <u>follow-up</u> calls between 4:30 and 5:00.** (*Follow-up* describes the calls.)
Functioning as a noun: **Scott is dogged when it comes to <u>follow-up</u>.** (*Follow-up* is a thing he is good at.)
Functioning as a verb and adverb: **Alec needs to <u>follow up</u> with Dr. McKee.** (He needs to *do* something: *follow up*.)

Tip #55

The hyphens in phrases like *well-deserved award* or *on-the-job training* help the reader, but drop the hyphens when the descriptive part follows whatever it is modifying.

The award was <u>well deserved</u> and, in fact, overdue.
Despite my extensive coursework, my most valuable learning occurred <u>on the job</u>.

Tip #56

Although it might look odd, this is correct:

The club is open to <u>13-</u> to <u>15-year-old</u> students. (Put a hyphen and a space after *13*; no hyphen after *to*.)

+ When dealing with words instead of numbers, the same rule applies.

  We offered the new benefit to full- and part-time employees.

  (But you might prefer *full-time and part-time employees* as less distracting and easier for the reader to process.)

Tip #57

A hyphen and a dash are entirely different punctuation marks. Hyphens mainly connect words, as in *last-minute change* or *fuel-saving idea*, while dashes mainly indicate that what follows is an interruption or a tangent to the main idea.

Hyphen: **Peter always was a risk-taker.**

En dash: **Biking on Runnymede Boulevard without a helmet is a risk – especially in this weather.**

Em dash: **Biking on Runnymede Boulevard without a helmet is a risk—especially in this weather.**

Tip #58

When you use a dash to set off a section, don't use a comma at the other end. You need to finish the job by inserting another dash or ending the sentence.

Incorrect: **After Steph flew to San Francisco—her first visit there in four years, she flew to a seminar in L.A.**

Correct: **After Steph flew to San Francisco—her first visit there in four years—she flew to a seminar in L.A.**

Correct: **Steph flew to San Francisco—her first visit there in four years.**

If you are considering earning a Ph.D. in dashes—or just want to know the difference between an *en dash* and an *em dash*—go to GPS #4.

UNDERSTANDING THE LAWS

Good drivers heed the rules of the road. They don't distract their passengers with transgressions that show carelessness and a poor grasp of fundamentals. Competent writers do the same for their readers.

Tip #59

Don't get seduced into making a fundamental grammar mistake because *I* and *myself* sound classier than *me*. Selecting a pronoun has nothing to do with style. Depending on what's happening in the sentence, one pronoun is correct and the rest aren't.

Tsk, tsk: **Please give your completed form to Barbara or I.**

Tsk, tsk again: **Please give your completed form to Barbara or myself.**

At last: **Please give your completed form to Barbara or me.**

+ Although some dilemmas about using *I*, *me*, or *myself* require grammar knowledge, this situation doesn't. Just apply the *rule of thumb*. If you read the sentence with your thumb over the words *Barbara or*, your ear will tell you *me* is correct. *Please give your completed form to I* and *Please give your completed form to myself* just don't sound right.

++ *Me* can be correct even when it is followed by a verb. Put your thumb over *my brother and* in this sentence to stay out of trouble.

Nope: **The Marshalls had my brother and I speak at the tribute event.** (The Marshalls had *I* speak?)

Yep: **The Marshalls had my brother and me speak at the tribute event.**

Tip #60

Agreement, such as subject-verb agreement, is a common cause of driving into a ditch.

Incorrect: **The set of books, exercises, and educational games were brilliantly conceived.** (Because several plural words separate the subject [*set*] and verb [*were*], it's easy to take your eye off the ball and get this wrong.)

Correct: **The set of books, exercises, and educational games was brilliantly conceived.**

Tip #61

Three nouns deserving particular attention when it comes to agreement are *agenda*, *media*, and *data*.

Agenda, though it's the plural of the Latin word *agendum*, is universally treated as singular. So we have no problem. In English *agenda* is singular and *agendas* is plural.

The agenda is shorter today.

Our agendas are developed by Tamar.

Media (plural of *medium*) is usually treated as plural, but sometimes we are not referring to a bunch of TV networks and newspapers; we are referring to the media as a collective whole.

Correct (because we mean many media outlets): **Our local <u>media haven't</u> let go of this issue.**
Correct (because we mean the media as one entity): **The <u>media seems</u> to be giving the new general manager the benefit of the doubt.**

Data (plural of *datum*) can also be treated as singular or plural, but, unlike *media*, it is usually seen as singular. When *data* refers to pieces of information, however, we should go plural.
Ambiguous context, so *data* is singular: **The <u>data demonstrates</u> that our promotions made an impact.**
Plural context because of *various*: **The <u>various data are</u> persuading me to change my mind.**

+ The treatment of words like *data* and others highlighted in GPS #5 is so sticky that editors and other experts can disagree. I have done my best to help you traverse these crossroads.

For more on this vexing matter of agreement, go to GPS #5.

Tip #62
Beware of sentences beginning with *There's*. This leads to a grammar mistake whenever what follows is plural.
Wrong: **<u>There's</u> several excellent applicants for the position.**
Right: **<u>There are</u> several excellent applicants for the position.**

+ Rephrasing sentences by dropping *There is* or *There are* often gives you the opportunity to use a dynamic verb or verb phrase instead of the commonplace verb *to be*. (For more on this point, see tip #100.)
Several excellent applicants <u>are vying</u> for the position.

Tip #63

Don't use the adjective *good* when you should use the adverb *well.*

Incorrect: **I thought he did good just to break even.**
Correct: **I thought he did well just to break even.**

+ When we're discussing how we feel (in terms of our physical health), *good* is grammatically correct and *well* is fully acceptable.

Correct: **I'm feeling good, thank you.**
Correct: **I'm feeling well, thank you.**
Correct: **I am good.**
Correct: **I am well.**

++ But when we use *feel* to mean our attitude, stick with the adjectives *good* and *bad* (as you would after other *linking verbs* like *seem* and *appear*).

Incorrect: **I feel well about our chances.**
Correct: **I feel good about our chances.**
Incorrect: **I feel badly about the misunderstanding.**
Correct: **I feel bad about the misunderstanding.**

Tip #64

Watch out for needlessly using *of* after other prepositions.

She lives inside (not *inside of*) **the city limits.**
I like having the water fountain right outside (not *outside of*) **my office.**
Pat lives off (not *off of*) **her pension.**

+ *Inside of* is correct, however, as a figure of speech meaning *in less than* or *fewer than*.

We should arrive before long—probably inside of an hour.
We're expecting inside of 100 people.

++ *Outside of* is correct as a figure of speech meaning *except* or *except for*.

Outside of regular maintenance, I've had no expenses.

Tip #65

The rules governing numbers are complex and subject to style. Here are a few generally accepted guidelines:

- Write out single-digit numbers and use numerals for 10 and above.

After 45 minutes of searching, she found the seven lost files.

- You can break the above rule for clarity.

The retreat was divided into three 2-hour sessions. (Putting *three* and *two-hour* together is more taxing for the reader.)

We are deploying volunteers in 18 twelve-person teams. (Same logic regarding *18 12-person teams.*)

- Write out numbers that begin a sentence, but use numerals for a year.

Fourteen members of our sales team attended the workshop.

2006 was a banner year for our firm. (If you are uncomfortable taking this license, just reword: *Our firm had a banner year in 2006.*)

- Use numerals for all ages, even those under 10.

My children are 6 and 8.

- When single-digit and double-digit numbers are used in a series, you may make them all numerals for uniformity.

We placed 13 orders on Wednesday, 10 on Thursday, and 8 on Friday. (But *eight on Friday* would be the choice of many writers and editors.)

Tip #66

When giving words initial caps in a title or heading, stay alert to short words like *Is*, *It*, *Be*, and *Put* that qualify for a capital letter. Yes, short words (fewer than four or five letters are standard rules of thumb) should be lowercase, but not when they are nouns, verbs, pronouns, adjectives, and adverbs—or the title's first or last word.

Incorrect capitalization: **Headquarters Expansion now set to Begin in March**

Correct capitalization: **Headquarters Expansion Now Set to Begin in March**

Incorrect capitalization: **Health Fair on for Friday: Talk it up**

Correct capitalization: **Health Fair on for Friday: Talk It Up**

+ Some emailers treat subject lines like titles, but deciding which words should get initial caps consumes time and leads to capitalization errors. (In *Subject: Need your Sales Figures by tonight*, why not *Your* and *Tonight*?) Save time and avoid trouble by using initial caps only for the first word of a subject line and words that are always capitalized like *Nashville* or *November*.

Subject: Need your sales figures by tonight

Tip #67

Seasons do not get initial caps.

We need to postpone our annual conference until spring.

Tip #68

North, *south*, *east*, and *west* get initial caps when they are places, but not as directions.

He has lived in the South his entire life.

Drive east for five miles and then turn north at Richmond Road.

Tip #69

Remember that the *superlative* form of an adjective is for comparisons of three or more.

Wrong: **Of the two candidates, Moore is clearly the <u>strongest</u>.**

Right: **Of the two candidates, Moore is clearly <u>stronger</u>.**

+ Parents often incorrectly refer to *my oldest child* or *my youngest child* even though they have just two children.

Tip #70

Watch out for *dangling modifiers.* Put a phrase that describes a person or thing directly before or after that person or thing.

Wrong (unless you are boasting about yourself): **<u>As an exemplary leader of our organization, I</u> invite you to serve as our next chair.**

Right: **I invite <u>you, as an exemplary leader of our organization</u>, to serve as our next chair.**

Right: **<u>As an exemplary leader of our organization, you</u> are invited to serve as our next chair.**

DRIVING WITH FINESSE

Drivers who know precisely where they are headed and manage their journey skillfully earn the confidence of their passengers.

Tip #71

Avoid adulterating the powerful word *unique* by putting a modifier like *very* or *rather* in front of it. *Unique* is an absolute word, meaning *one-of-a-kind*. *Very one-of-a-kind* and *rather one-of-a-kind* don't make sense.

+ You can, however, use a modifier like *truly* with *unique*.

 Esther came up with a truly unique approach.

Tip #72

If you overuse *very* when you write, you might need to aim for more freshness and precision. *Very* often signifies that the next word is inadequate.

 Her comments were very good. (Ho-hum.)
 Her comments were excellent. (Or *superb* or *terrific* or *outstanding*, etc. This is stronger, but why were her comments excellent?)
 Her comments were eye-opening and inspiring. (Aha!)

Tip #73

Avoid writing formal words and phrases like *herewith*, *pursuant to*, *accordingly*, *I am in receipt of*, *enclosed please find*, and *attached please find* if you would not use them when speaking. Readers should feel that you are talking to them.

> Unnatural, stuffy tone: **I am in receipt of your June 17 inquiry and will respond forthwith upon our executive director's return from vacation.**
>
> Natural, informal tone: **I received your June 17 letter and will get back to you as soon as our executive director returns from vacation.**

+ *Enclosed please find* and *attached please find* rob you of the opportunity to use *I* or *we*. Why pass up the opportunity to reinforce your connection with the reader?

> Formulaic and impersonal: **<u>Enclosed please find</u> our latest company brochure.**
>
> Natural and personal: **<u>I have enclosed</u> our latest company brochure.**

Tip #74

Have a reason for using *passive voice* instead of *active voice*. (In passive voice the emphasis is on the action, not the performer of the action.) One of several reasons to use passive voice is to conceal information.

> Active voice: **Jason <u>misplaced</u> one of the boxes of invitations.** (The culprit has been revealed.)
>
> Passive voice: **One of the boxes of invitations <u>was misplaced</u>.** (Jason has been protected.)

+ The occasional use of passive voice can also enhance rhythm and add a bit of drama to our writing.

> **All the information in these reports was gathered, distilled,**

verified, and summarized by Nancy. (We had to wait until the end of the sentence to find out who performed all the valuable work.)

++ Passive voice is especially useful in writing minutes or informal meeting summaries. That way the action takes center stage while allowing participants to maintain anonymity.

A suggestion was made to designate prime parking spaces for the management team. When concerns were raised about the effect of preferential parking on overall morale, the idea was abandoned.

+++ Note that passive voice verbs are always *verb phrases* (*was misplaced*, *were raised*, etc.). Verb phrases can be a clue that you are unintentionally writing in passive voice when you might prefer to be in active voice. (Not all verb phrases are passive, but all passive voice sentences contain verb phrases.)

Tip #75

Don't be uncomfortable if you are writing shorter sentences on the job than you did in school. You might even want to pat yourself on the back. In a term paper or essay exam, crafting complex sentences might have exhibited mastery of writing and the course content, but in the workplace most readers are in a hurry. Leaning toward shorter sentences can reap the triple-benefit of pleasing readers, enhancing clarity, and helping to avoid grammar errors.

+ At times you will need longer sentences, of course, to convey more information or simply to vary the rhythm. Longer sentences particularly pay off at the beginning of an email or other document as you *frame* the message for your reader. Remember the principle of the *thesis sentence* from English class?

Tip #76

In school we were not allowed to write sentence fragments because our teachers needed to make sure we understood the difference between a complete sentence and an incomplete one. But with maturity come privileges. If you have recovered from the school days prohibition and are comfortable dropping in an occasional fragment for impact or rhythm, go for it. Anything to keep our readers engaged. (See, I just did it.)

Do you agree that the fragments ending these statements add punch?

> **If you give me all the information, I can get you a quote this week. <u>Probably by Thursday.</u>**
>
> **I just figured out who's replacing Sam. <u>No one.</u>**
>
> **Please confine your summary to a page or less. <u>Preferably, a lot less.</u>**

Tip #77

Don't shy away from constructing a paragraph containing just one sentence. Short paragraphs are generally much more effective than those that pack together too much information. (Teachers might have justifiably admonished us for writing one-sentence paragraphs because they were looking for us to support our points, but readers opening 100 emails a day don't want depth in every message. Besides, smartphone users appreciate white space.)

Tip #78

Don't twist yourself in knots to avoid ending a sentence with a preposition. We're allowed to end a sentence with a preposition—especially when doing otherwise will sound unnatural.

Awkward: **I'm not sure <u>from where</u> this suggestion came.**
Fine: **I'm not sure where this suggestion came <u>from</u>.**

+ If ending with a preposition sounds weak, and you can comfortably rearrange the phrasing, do so.
Acceptable: **Please hand your registration <u>in</u>.**
Better: **Please hand <u>in</u> your registration.**

Tip #79

Splitting an infinitive means putting a word between *to* and the verb that goes with it (*to boldly go*). Playing strictly by the rules, we're supposed to avoid splitting an infinitive—unless rewording will sound awkward—but most readers will not notice or object to our taking this liberty. So this is an admonition from our school days we can largely dismiss.

But if you are writing someone who might get distracted by this minor infraction, or you are writing a more formal document and want to be on your best behavior, just rearrange the words.
Split infinitive: **I want <u>to temporarily halt</u> this discussion.**
The repair job: **I want <u>to halt</u> this discussion <u>temporarily</u>.**

Notice, however, that on occasion rearranging isn't the answer.
To truly understand your idea, I need more background. (Where else can *truly* go and sound natural? Here you need to let the split infinitive stand or reinvent the sentence.)

+ Note that splitting a *verb phrase* (like *should recover* or *may attend*) is not the same as splitting an infinitive (like *to discover* or *to examine*). We should always feel comfortable putting an adverb inside a verb phrase.
I hope I <u>can quickly answer</u> the question you raised in the meeting. (*Quickly* works best between *can* and *answer*.)

Tip #80

Contrary to what you might have been instructed in school—or what you *think* you were instructed—you may begin sentences with *And* and *But*. *Because* is another effective way to begin your point.

> **<u>And</u> we lost our next three games.**
> **<u>But</u> we won the season finale in extra innings.**
> **<u>Because</u> of our dramatic win in the last game, we made the playoffs.**

+ Suppress the impulse to place a comma after an opening *And* or *But*. It's true that when speaking we sometimes pause momentarily for drama (*And … that will always remain a mystery*), but that doesn't give us a reason to stick a comma after *And*.

> No: **And, I never missed another class.**
> Yes: **And I never missed another class.**
> Yes: **And, despite my demanding work schedule, I never missed another class.** (Here the comma is correct because *despite my demanding work schedule* needs commas on both sides.)

Tip #81

Impact, as a substitute for *make an impact*, is on the hit list of many exacting writers who reserve the verb *impact* for a collision. (*The rocket shell impacted the wall of the hospital.*)

> Not recommended: **Sydney's rousing speech <u>impacted</u> her team.**
> Recommended: **Sydney's rousing speech <u>made an impact</u> on her team.**

+ Even *made an impact* can often be improved by more precise wording.

> **Sydney's rousing speech <u>inspired</u> her team.**
> **Sydney's rousing speech <u>prodded</u> her team to play with renewed determination.**

++ On the subject of objectionable verbs, some readers object to *new verbs*, such as *incentivize*, that have morphed from nouns. Handle with care.

Tip #82

Writing looks smoother and more sophisticated without needless capitalization. When in doubt, don't capitalize. Most reasons to use capital letters are obvious.

Heavy-handed: **I used the Suggestion Box to submit my ideas on Flexible Hours.**

Refined: **I used the suggestion box to submit my ideas on flexible hours.**

+ A tough capitalization call regards job titles. Strictly speaking, titles should receive initial caps only when they directly precede names, but many businesses and organizations do not follow this rule. You need to know the culture of your workplace.

We invited President Chloe Tyler to open the meeting. (Always correct.)

Send your suggestions to Chloe Tyler, president of our firm. (Correct, but maybe not the style in your workplace. See tip #87 for more on consistent style.)

Tip #83

Don't carelessly use *literally* just for emphasis; use it when your words are actual.

Probably not: **I literally laughed my head off.**

Quite possible: **The drug reaction made him literally afraid of his shadow.**

Tip #84

Substituting *hopefully* for *I hope* or *we hope* is frowned upon by some experts. For sure, *hopefully* isn't as personal and direct.

Noncommittal: **Hopefully, you'll win the award.**

Committed: **I hope you win the award.**

+ *Hopefully* is better used to mean *with hope*.

She talked to us about her illness honestly and hopefully.

Tip #85

Using language like *soon* or *ASAP* (or *asap*) gives messages urgency but doesn't fully communicate. Does *soon* mean in 15 minutes or by tomorrow? If time is the issue, be specific.

I need your report today by 5:30 p.m.

+ Beware of *ASAP* affecting your tone. It can sound overly demanding.

Tip #86

Don't waffle. Words and phrases like *somewhat*, *rather*, and *a bit* are fine if you really mean them, but when you are truly frustrated don't mislead by writing that you are *fairly frustrated*. Write with conviction. And the phrases *kind of* and *sort of* can be discarded altogether.

+ Sometimes we are redundant because we have expressed uncertainty twice in the same sentence.

Fat: **I'm guessing this adjustment will probably do the trick.**

Lean: **I'm guessing this adjustment will do the trick.**

Leaner: **This adjustment will probably do the trick.**

Leanest: **This adjustment should do the trick.**

Tip #87
Consider creating a personal *style guide*. Some employers have a style guide to help ensure consistency and correctness among all workers, but most don't. That shouldn't stop you, however, from maintaining your own. For example, you might have decided that you prefer *email* to *e-mail*, *theater* to *theatre*, *chair* to *chairperson*, *Davis's* to *Davis'*, and *stamping ground* to *stomping ground*. If you keep a mental or written list of these choices, you'll save a few seconds of decision-making from time to time and, more important, avoid distracting your reader with inconsistencies.

+ You may also want to create a style guide for a particular document. Let's say several members of your department have written sections for a new benefits brochure, and you are responsible for editing the copy. Program your antennae to catch potential inconsistencies like *health care* vs. *healthcare* and *adviser* vs. *advisor*. Also be on the lookout for inconsistencies like en dashes vs. em dashes or italicized vs. bold headings.

++ A source of inconsistent writing in virtually any workplace is the *serial comma*. That's because both of the following are correct:

> **We're looking for a new marketing assistant, events manager and sales associate.** (No comma after *manager*.)
> **We're looking for a new marketing assistant, events manager, and sales associate.** (Comma after *manager*.)

I chose to use the serial comma in this handbook, but I could just as easily have omitted the optional serial comma. If you have been in the dark about the serial comma since fifth grade, see GPS #6 for illumination.

Tip #88

When you use bullets, *parallel construction* lends refinement to your writing and gets the reader into a consistent rhythm. So if the first bullet is a phrase beginning with an *-ing* word like *Organizing*, the following bullets should begin with other *-ing* words like *Focusing*, *Executing*, and *Evaluating*.

We need to do the following:

- **Invite Joyce to chair the task force.**
- **Select one person per department to serve with her.**
- **Establishment of date for first meeting.** (Oops. Stay in rhythm with *Establish date for first meeting*.)

+ A common lapse in parallelism is presenting some bullets as full sentences and some as sentence fragments. This inconsistency can distract the reader and appear to be a mistake.

++ Also watch out for lack of parallelism within a sentence.

I need you to give a brief presentation, create complementary visuals and a one-page handout. (The parallelism breaks down because there is no verb for *a one-page handout*.)

Fix A: If the verb *create* is doing double-duty, delete the comma and insert *and*.

I need you to <u>give</u> a brief presentation <u>and create</u> complementary visuals and a one-page handout.

Fix B: If *create* refers only to the *complementary visuals*, you need a verb to go with *one-page handout*.

I need you to <u>give</u> a brief presentation, <u>create</u> complementary visuals, and <u>develop</u> a one-page handout.

Tip #89

When bulleted items are complete sentences, use a period after each. That's what your reader expects. If they are not sentences, ending with a period or omitting punctuation both work fine

Here are my suggestions for the agenda:

- **We need to discuss the new logo ideas.**
- **Eric has preliminary survey results.**
- **Lil should review the timeline for the online contest.**

Here are my suggestions for the agenda:

- **New logo ideas**
- **Preliminary survey results**
- **Timeline for online contest**

Tip #90

Although brevity is a worthy goal, relax your impulse to be concise when composing subject lines of emails and memos. Help the reader assign importance to your message.

Vague: **Subject: Security**

Much more helpful: **Subject: New sign-in procedure begins May 1**

+ When responding to an email, refocus the subject line if the change will give the reader a head start. Let's say the organizer of an event sent all colleagues extensive information with the subject line *Need help with September 6 all-day fair*. You are responding because you can help staff a booth from 1 to 3. Many responses, made for a variety of reasons, will simply say *Re: Need help with September 6 all-day fair*. Your subject line will stand out and help the recipient if it says something like *Gotcha covered 1–3*.

Tip #91

Beware of the few words in our language that can be understood in opposite ways. For example, a *quota* could be a minimum or a maximum. *Downhill* could indicate that something went awry or that it became effortless.

> Ambiguous: **The parents protested the softball league's quota regarding 10-year-olds.** (Does the league want more 10-year-olds to play or fewer?)
>
> Clear: **The parents protested the softball league's ceiling of five 10-year-olds per team.**
>
> Ambiguous: **After Barry delivered his witty opening remarks, it was downhill from there.** (Was he coasting or did the speech fall apart?)
>
> Clear: **After Barry delivered his witty opening remarks, the audience couldn't get enough of him.**

+ Watch out as well for using a word in two ways close together, which can distract the reader.

> Change recommended: **Inez is heading the project to position herself as a candidate for the new marketing position.**
>
> Resolved: **Inez is heading the project to position herself as a candidate for the new opportunity in marketing.**

Tip #92

Spelling matters. A spelling error can distract your reader and rob you of credibility. Moreover, if it's obvious you didn't take the time to run your message through your spell-checking device, the reader might be offended by your laxness.

+ Commonly misspelled words include *accommodate*, *liaison*, *curiosity*, *memento*, *millennium*, *privilege*, *supersede*, and *led*.

++ Be especially careful with the name of the person you are writing. Double-check to make sure *John* isn't *Jon* and *Brown* isn't *Browne*.

Tip #93

Should we put one space between sentences or two? It doesn't matter in terms of correctness, but the modern style is to use one. Two spaces was the norm in the days of typewriting because spacing between letters was inconsistent, and a narrow letter like *i* or *l* had a lot of space around it. Two spaces between sentences gave readers a more substantial visual break. In the digital age, with uniform spaces between letters, one space does the job—but you could encounter a particular document that calls for two spaces by convention or because of a design decision.

Tip #94

Although your writing should sound natural, watch out for overused and vague adjectives like *awesome*, *amazing*, *incredible*, and *tremendous*. They can make writing seem less professional, and they may not be saying enough.

Vague: **The staff retreat was <u>tremendous</u>.**

Informative: **The staff retreat was <u>entertaining</u> and quite <u>helpful</u> in revising year-end goals.**

Tip #95

Consider being creative—like a headline writer—when using headings. Instead of simply titling the first section of a report *Introduction* or *Background*, you can communicate much more and draw in the reader with *Sales Projections Turn Optimistic* or *Chronic Turnover Emerges as Key Challenge*.

Tip #96
Noticing that certain language is getting a lot of play does not mean you are missing the boat if you don't sprinkle some into your own writing. To the contrary, readers appreciate fresh language that does not rely on trendy or overworked words and phrases like *parameters*, *iconic*, *robust*, *solutions*, *strategic*, *at the end of the day*, *going forward*, *step up to the plate*, and *outside the box*.

+ *Parameters* can be especially irksome to scientific types who know the word is misused as a synonym for *guidelines* or *boundaries*. If you mean *guidelines*, say it.

Tip #97
Only is a slippery word. We tend to drop it in right before the verb—even when it doesn't really belong there—so occasionally we should move *only* to clarify our meaning.

Ambiguous: **We <u>only reviewed</u> sales figures in the morning.** (Taken literally, this would seem to mean that the sales figures were *only reviewed* when more could have happened. For example, the figures could have been analyzed statistically. But the real meaning is probably one of the following two.)

Clear: **We reviewed <u>only sales figures</u> in the morning.** (We could have gone over other data—such as expenses—but only sales figures were discussed.)

Clear: **We reviewed sales figures <u>only in the morning</u>.** (The topic of sales figures did not come up in the afternoon.)

+ Even when the meaning is clear, see if *only* is in the right spot.

I only watched two episodes. (Let's make a move.)
I watched only two episodes. (Good move!)

Tip #98

Although the percent symbol certainly belongs in charts, writing out *percent* in sentences can add a touch of elegance.

> **Our new overtime policy helped productivity rise 11 percent.**

Tip #99

Think twice about using *former*, *latter*, and *respectively*. They often burden the reader unnecessarily.

> Cumbersome: **If you're asking me to choose between the corner room with a view of the city and the large, first-floor room off the lobby, I vote for the former.**
>
> Straightforward: **If you're asking me to choose between the corner room with a view of the city and the large, first-floor room off the lobby, I vote for the room with a view.**
>
> Cumbersome: **She's presenting at a three-day journalism conference and a CFO leadership retreat in Detroit and Chicago, respectively.**
>
> Straightforward: **She's presenting at a three-day journalism conference in Detroit and a CFO leadership retreat in Chicago.**

Tip #100

The verb *to be*, in all its forms, is the verb we use the most, but it adds no zest to our writing. Replace *is*, *was*, *were*, *have been*, and all the rest with action verbs when you can.

> Drab: **This year's campaign result was better than last year's.**
>
> Dynamic: **This year's campaign result surpassed** (or *exceeded* or *eclipsed*) **last year's.**

Avoiding Wrong Turns

What a relief to rely on our GPS when we're feeling lost. To get past a few particularly challenging situations, here is some guidance.

GPS Guidance #1—Affect vs. Effect

Plenty of intelligent people start to perspire when struggling with *affect* and *effect*. As noted in tip #7, if you happen to be good at grammar, it helps to keep in mind that *affect* is usually a verb—meaning to *influence* or to *make an impact on*. *Effect* is usually a noun—meaning a *result*. If you're not strong in grammar, here are three tricks to help distinguish between the two words:

- Use alphabetical order. *Affect* comes before *effect*, and first you need to *affect* someone or something to make an *effect* on that person or thing.
- Line up the *a* in *affect* with the *a* in *act*; the *e* in *effect* with the *e* in *end*. When you *affect* someone or something you are *acting*—taking *action*. The *effect* is the *end* you have achieved.
- Remember that *result* has an *e* but no *a*, and an *effect* is a *result*.

But why do I say that *affect* is usually a verb and *effect* usually a noun?

Affect (accent on the first syllable) is also a noun that refers to one's demeanor or mood.

> **I was glad to see Noah showing a much brighter affect this morning.**

Effect is also a verb that means to put into effect or to make happen.

> **Management is effecting a more generous sick day policy.** (Management isn't *affecting* the policy [influencing it]; management is putting a new policy in place. So the verb *effect* often relates to implementing new laws, policies, or procedures.)

GPS Guidance #2—Lie vs. Lay

As if choosing between the verbs *lie* and *lay* weren't hard enough, as noted in tip #11, the past tense of *lie* is *lay* (not *laid*). This point catches almost everyone by surprise. *The baby laid quietly in her crib after her nap* might sound right, but the unnatural-sounding *The baby lay quietly* is correct. So here is the conjugation of the two verbs:

> *Lie*, present tense: **I need to lie down for a while.** (Not *lay*.)
> *Lie*, past tense: **Yesterday I lay on the sofa all afternoon watching sports.** (Not *laid*.)
> *Lie*, past participle: **She has lain in bed since noon listening to music.** (Not *has laid*.)
>
> *Lay*, present tense: **Please lay down that book and get ready to leave.**
> *Lay*, past tense: **I can't remember where I laid my tickets.**
> *Lay*, past participle: **The workers have laid their tools all over the yard.**

+ Note that most of us get the conjugations of *lay* (*lay*, *laid*, *have* or *has laid*) right just by using what sounds natural. It's the three conjugations of *lie* (*lie*, *lay*, *have* or *has lain*) that challenge us.

++ An inanimate object can *lie* as well.

Don't let the hose lie (not *lay*) **where someone can trip over it.**

I found your sweater lying (not *laying*) **next to the sofa.**

+++ The conjugation of the other verb *lie* (to tell a falsehood) is just what it would seem:

Today I lie, yesterday I lied, and I have lied.

GPS Guidance #3—Who vs. Whom

I hope the trick noted in tip #15 is helpful, but the *who/whom* dilemma is really tough for three reasons:

- Many perfectly respectable people never say *whom*, so our ears don't help us. We have to rely on our grammar rules.
- The grammar—even for those unafraid to go there—is not easy. First you need to understand *subjective* and *objective* case and recognize that pronouns like *who*, *whoever*, *I*, *we*, *he*, *she*, and *they* are subjective; *whom*, *whomever*, *me*, *us*, *him*, *her*, and *them* are objective. That means when a pronoun is an *object of a preposition*, *direct object*, or *indirect object*, you'd use *whom*.
  I don't know for whom this was intended.
  You invited whom?
- Even when we know we're right, using *whom* can sound pretentious.

Here's my advice: When writing informally (you'll have to decide where to draw the line), feel comfortable making your go-to pronoun *who*.

That's what most of us say, so emailing *I finally decided who to send to the conference* won't distract many readers even though *whom* is correct. But at other times you may want to pause and apply the *he/him* trick from tip #15 to get it right.

Now what about *whoever* vs. *whomever*? Let's say your sentence in a more formal or important document is *We will award the box seats to whoever/whomever sells the most raffle tickets*. You might think this is clearly objective case (object of the preposition *to*), making the correct choice *whomever*. Not so fast. Use the trick to choose the pronoun that works as the subject of *sells the most raffle tickets*. Would you say *He sells* or *Him sells*? Clearly, it would be *He*, which aligns with *whoever*.

> **We will award the box seats to whoever sells the most raffle tickets.**

But it would be *whomever* in *I'm giving the box seats to whomever Marcia picks as salesperson-of-the-week*. That's because you'd say *Marcia picks him as salesperson-of-the-week*. *Whomever* aligns with *him*.

Whew. This is why it often pays to reword a sentence rather than struggle with a difficult choice. So you could change *I finally decided who/whom to send to the conference* to *I finally decided who's going to the conference*. In that construction you can rely on your ear. (Or you could be less mysterious: *I finally decided to ask Jerry to go to the conference*.)

GPS Guidance #4—Dashes vs. Hyphens

One of the difficulties of this fork in the road, mentioned in tips #57 and #58, is that many writers don't even see the fork. If you use the words *dash* and *hyphen* interchangeably, your writing probably reflects this failure to distinguish between the two punctuation marks.

The hyphen isn't mysterious. We know how to use it (e.g., in a phrase like *life-changing moment*) and where to find it (on the keyboard's upper right). The dash, however, is mysterious on both counts. When might we use it, and where the heck is it?

A principal reason to use a dash in everyday writing is to alert the reader that you are interrupting yourself or going off on a tangent—in much the same way that we might enclose words in parentheses. See, I just used one. Here are two more examples:

> **We are sending four representatives—all from our fiscal department—to the seminar.**
>
> **I never had time to proof the report—not that I'd have caught the one minor error anyway.**

If you get the gist of when we might take advantage of this useful and stylish punctuation mark—and you have been persuaded that you shouldn't ask a hyphen to perform the dash's job—you now want to know how to make it. That's a bit complicated because you need to choose between an *em dash* and an *en dash*.

The em dash, which I have been using in this book, got its name in the old days of typography because it was roughly the width of the letter *m*. You can probably now guess how the en dash got its name. Take a look at each:

> Em dash: **I was thrilled we won the trophy—especially given our slow start.**
>
> En dash: **I was thrilled we won the trophy – especially given our slow start.**

In most newspapers, magazines, and books, you'll see the em dash in this instance, but an en dash is acceptable (and the choice of my hometown newspaper). Pick the one you like and be consistent.

Before we reveal how to make the two dashes, note the following:

- An em dash virtually touches the letters on either side.
- An en dash has one space on either side when used in this way. (The other way to use an en dash is coming up.)
- A hyphen has no spaces around it (as in *daughter-in-law*).

Software varies, but you can make an em dash by pressing the hyphen key twice. When you make the space after the following word, a magic trick should happen. The double-hyphen (--) turns into a true em dash(—). On any computer, if you go to *Help* and enter *dash*, you should find a shortcut.

You can make an en dash by pressing space, hyphen, hyphen, space. Again, the magic won't happen until you type the next word and a space. (Most likely, you will get the same result with space, hyphen, space.) Go to *Help* for the en dash shortcut.

We're nearly done. Remember I said a few paragraphs ago that there is another way to use an en dash? First decide if this looks okay:

I met her sometime during my 1998-1999 school year.

I imagine it looks fine, but I'll split hairs to point out that this use of a hyphen for *to* or *through* should really be an en dash with no spaces:

I met her sometime during my 1998–1999 school year.

Okay, one more fine point: Even if you know to use an en dash instead of a hyphen when dealing with dates, you're not exactly right in this example:

I believe she served as ambassador from 2004–2008. (The hairsplitting issue here is that the companion of *from* is *to*, not an en dash. So both of the following are correct:)

> **She served as ambassador from 2004 to 2008.**
> **She served as 2004–2008 ambassador.**

You now nearly qualify for your Ph.D. in dashes. You'll just need to pick a dissertation topic.

GPS #5—Agreement

Getting verbs to agree with subjects and getting pronouns to agree with nouns might be the toughest grammatical issue we face. Agreement is a nemesis because we can go wrong for several reasons:

- Meandering sentences.

  As noted in tip #60, sometimes we slip because by the time we get to the verb we have "lost the scent." Losing track of whether the subject is singular or plural can occur easily, as in this sentence:
  The instructions to the game, mailed to everyone a week before the party, was all we needed to feel like experts.

  What's the subject of the sentence? *Instructions* (plural). And the verb? *Was* (singular). Oops. Better make a correction.
  The instructions to the game, mailed to everyone a week before the party, were all we needed to feel like experts.

- Collective nouns.

  Several nouns, like *group*, *staff*, and *couple*, pose problems because they can be singular or plural depending on the context. (And as noted earlier, collective nouns are so hard to handle that some experts and editorial boards might disagree about agreement. Nevertheless, I will bravely forge ahead.)

Which is correct?
The group is addressing that issue right now.
The group are addressing that issue right now. (I'd use the singular *is* because the group is seen as a whole.)

But what if the group is expressed as a number of individuals?
The group of professors was quite varied in its opinions.
The group of professors were quite varied in their opinions. (Here I'd switch to the plurals, *were* and *their*, because the professors are hardly a unit.)

How about this one?
The staff applauded themselves for surpassing the sales goal.
The staff applauded itself for surpassing the sales goal. (The context makes *staff applauded themselves* seem right, but in the following I'd treat *staff* as singular:)
Our staff is excellent.

So I would consider this correct:
The couple is vacationing in Hawaii. (The couple is seen as a unit.)

And this:
The couple are arguing over where to go on vacation. (The two members of the couple are not unified in their views.)

Because these decisions can be so troublesome, we can often save time and make sure we're right by rewording. For example, changing *staff* to *staff members* solves the example above.
The staff members applauded themselves for surpassing the sales goal.

- Three special cases: *company*, *everyone*, and *none*.

Company is not ambiguous; it's singular. But in the workplace we often see sentences such as this:
The company had their annual picnic yesterday.

Because we think of a company as a collection of many people, *their* is passable, but it isn't really correct. This is:
The company had its annual picnic yesterday.

Once again, rewording can eliminate the dilemma:
The company employees had their annual picnic yesterday.

Which of these is your choice?
Everyone needs to complete their profile by Friday.
Everyone needs to complete his profile by Friday.

Trick question. The first choice is flawed because *everyone* is singular and *their* is plural, and the second choice is politically incorrect. Once upon a time *everyone* took the pronoun *his*, but that's a no-no now that we want to be gender-neutral. So we could do this: *Everyone needs to complete his or her* (or *his/her*) *profile by Friday*. But both of those choices are clumsy.

A better solution is making the context plural so you can use *their* correctly:
All employees need to complete their profiles by Friday.

What about *none*? Is it singular or plural? Another trick question. It can be either. When *none* means *not one*, it's singular.
Of all my colleagues, none (not one) **is as impressive as Suzanne.**

And when *none* means *not any*, we need to consider context.
None (not any) **of the trouble** (singular) **was my fault.**

None (not any) **of the troubles** (plural) **are serious.**

Now you can reward yourself with a scoop of ice cream or mindless TV show. You just survived the book's most taxing issue.

GPS Guidance #6—The Serial Comma

As established in tip #87, when commas separate three or more items, the *serial comma* is optional. Either of these is correct:

Her kids were born in June, July and August.
Her kids were born in June, July, and August.

So what's the problem? We can't go wrong, right? Well, there's more to this. For openers, you want to be consistent in using or omitting the serial comma—if not over your entire life, at least for the life of an important document.

So let's say you prefer to omit the optional serial comma. What are you going to do with this sentence?

I need three more invitations for Sebastian and Lola, Judah and Ariel and Rosie.

Because you decided you prefer to omit the serial comma, your reader doesn't know if Ariel is being invited with Judah or with Rosie. A serial comma clears the confusion: *I need three more invitations for Sebastian and Lola, Judah, and Ariel and Rosie*. Or … *I need three more invitations for Sebastian and Lola, Judah and Ariel, and Rosie.*

Aha. Then using the serial comma all the time makes sense, right? Not really. Consider this sentence:

We invited Dee Smith, the CFO, and Dick Jones.

Is Dee the CFO, or is the CFO a third party? Were three people invited or two? We don't know. But if we happen to know the writer *doesn't* use the serial comma, we know the comma after *CFO* signifies that this is Dee's title. Two people were invited. Hmm. So maybe the advantage has just swung back to omitting the serial comma.

What's the solution? If you want to write in the style of most modern publications, omit the serial comma and know that you'll need to stray from your personal style in a sentence like the one about the three invitations. If you believe that clarity should trump a cleaner look, use the serial comma because it more often enhances comprehension. Just know that on occasion you'll need to rewrite a sentence like the CFO one:

> **We invited Dee Smith, Dick Jones, and the CFO** (three people).
> **We invited CFO Dee Smith and Dick Jones** (two people).

In this book I chose to use the serial comma, even though the other style is more prevalent. (What a rebel!) If you now realize you are inconsistent in using the serial comma, try one style for a while and see how you like it.

GPS #7 The Recommended Road

As demonstrated through these concluding issues, some matters of correctness are tough to solve and might even draw conflicting answers from different experts. So recognize that we all make errors. Just try to get better each year at limiting them and avoiding the major missteps that can undermine credibility. And remember, rewording to avoid a thorny grammar or punctuation issue is not wimpy. It's smart.

INDEX (by tip number)

INDEX (by tip number) CONT'D

INDEX (by tip number) CONT'D

About the Author

Norm's writing and communications career spans more than 30 years. His articles have appeared in the *New York Times*, *Plain Dealer*, and many other publications. In the past 15 years he has led hundreds of workshops—from New York to LA—on writing in the workplace.

Norm earned a B.A. in psychology from Miami University and an M.A. in communications from Ohio State. He and his wife live in Shaker Heights, Ohio.

"This book is the product of a lifetime of paying attention to how others express themselves," Norm says, "and decades of working to perfect my writing and help others refine theirs."

For more background, visit www.normfriedman.com.